MY FIRST LOOK AT SCIENCE

WOODPECKERS MAKE NOISE BY TAPPING ON WOOD

Sound

MELISSA GISH

CREATIVE EDUCATION

Published by Creative Education

123 South Broad Street, Mankato, Minnesota 56001

Creative Education is an imprint of The Creative Company

Designed by Rita Marshall

Photographs by Joan Balzarini, Corbis (Mathias Kulka, Tim McGuire), Getty Images (C.

Wolcott Henery III/National Geographic, John Miller, Darren Robb, Michael Wildsmith),

Roy Gumpel, Gregory M. Nelson

Cover illustration © 1996 Roberto Innocenti

Copyright © 2006 Creative Education

Printed in the United States of America

Library of Congress Cataloging-in-Publication Data

Gish, Melissa. Sound / by Melissa Gish.

p. cm. — (My first look at science)

Includes index.

ISBN 1-58341-374-X

I. Sound—Juvenile literature. I. Title. II. Series.

QC225.5.G535 2005   534—dc22   2004055262

First edition 9 8 7 6 5 4 3 2 1

Sound

SPEEDY SOUND

Sound is made when objects **vibrate**. When you talk or sing, part of your throat vibrates. This creates what we call sound.

Sound moves through the air fast. It goes about 1,115 feet (340 m) in just one second. That's 12 times faster than a car on the highway! Sound moves even faster through water or solid objects like wood.

AIRPLANES ARE LOUD WHEN THEY TAKE OFF

Wires are used to carry sound very quickly. When we talk on the telephone, the sound seems to get to the other person's telephone right away.

Pitch

Sounds move kind of like the waves on the ocean. But unlike water waves, we cannot see sound waves. Only our **eardrums** can feel them.

Sound moves through
steel 15 times faster
than it moves through the air.

THESE TELEPHONE WIRES CARRY SOUNDS

WHEN A STRING VIBRATES, IT MAKES SOUND

Pitch is the word we use to describe differences in sounds. Is the pitch high, like a bird singing? Or is it low, like thunder? A high-pitched sound is made when an object vibrates very quickly. A low-pitched sound is made when an object vibrates slowly.

The blue whale is

the loudest animal.

Its noises can be heard

530 miles (850 km) away!

BLUE WHALES MAKE LOW-PITCHED SOUNDS

Many sounds cannot be heard by humans. A dog can hear some high-pitched whistles that people cannot hear. Insects can hear some low-pitched sounds that people cannot hear.

Making Music

Musical instruments use different kinds of vibrations to make sounds. When you hit a drum, the drum vibrates slowly. This makes a low-pitched sound. When you blow into a recorder, it makes a special part vibrate quickly. This makes a high-pitched sound.

DOGS CAN HEAR HIGH-PITCHED SOUNDS

The strings of a guitar vibrate when you pluck them. This makes a musical sound, too. You can make music with almost anything that makes noise!

Measuring Sound

We measure how long something is using inches. We measure how much something weighs using pounds. The loudness of sound can be measured, too. We measure sound using decibels.

THE BIGGER THE DRUM, THE LOUDER THE SOUND

A whisper is about 20 decibels. A normal speaking voice is about 55 decibels. Every time you add 10 decibels, the sound is 10 times louder. A **subway train** is 90 decibels. That's loud. But a jet taking off is 120 decibels. That's 1,000 times louder than the subway train! Sounds that are loud can be heard very far away.

The decibel system

was **invented** by

Alexander Graham Bell.

He invented the telephone, too.

A PICTURE OF ALEXANDER GRAHAM BELL

Sound is all around us. Cars zoom by. Dogs bark. Kids shout. Sound lets us make music and talk to each other. What would the world be like without sound?

Sometimes sounds hit
something and bounce
back to our ears.
What we hear is called an echo.

Hands-on: Sound Vibrations

You can see and hear how vibration makes sound with this experiment.

What You Need

A plastic drinking glass
A rubber band

What You Do

1. Stretch the rubber band around the glass (top to bottom).
2. With one finger, strum the rubber band across the top of the glass. This makes the rubber band vibrate.
3. Hold the bottom of the glass to your ear. Strum the rubber band again. The sound made by the vibrating rubber band is louder because it is closer to your eardrum.

THE STRINGS OF A VIOLIN VIBRATE TO MAKE MUSIC

Index

Words to Know

eardrums—parts inside your ears that vibrate when sound waves hit them

invented—created or built for the first time

subway train—a train that runs under the ground

vibrate—to quickly move back and forth or up and down

Read More

Levine, Shar, and Leslie Johnstone. *Science of Sound and Music*. New York: Sterling Publishing, 2002.

Pfeffer, Wendy. *Sounds All Around*. New York: HarperCollins, 1999.

Royston, Angela. *Sound and Hearing*. Chicago: Heinemann Library, 2002.

Explore the Web

A Science Odyssey: Radio Transmission
http://www.pbs.org/wgbh/aso/tryit/radio/

Sound and Noise http://www.fatlion.com/science/sound.html

The Sound Site http://www.sci.mus.mn.us/sound/nocss/top.html